COOK
AS
I
SAY,
NOT
AS
I
DO

—

Margaret Sullivan

—

CHICAGO REVIEW PRESS

Remember Sada Nakamura . . .

Library of Congress Cataloging-in-Publication Data

Sullivan, Margaret   (Margaret Teresa)
    Cook as I say, not as I do / Margaret Sullivan.
       p.   cm.
    ISBN 1-55652-224-X   : $12.95
    1. Cookery.   2. Cookery—Humor.   I. Title.
TX714.S83   1994
641.5—dc20   94-30348
                                                CIP

© 1995 by Margaret Sullivan
First edition
Published by Chicago Review Press, Incorporated
814 North Franklin Street, Chicago, Illinois, 60610
Printed in the United States of America
ISBN 1-55652-224-X

1 2 3 4 5 6 7 8 9 10

"Think of how amazing it is that you even got here."

—Norm Holly

The Recipes

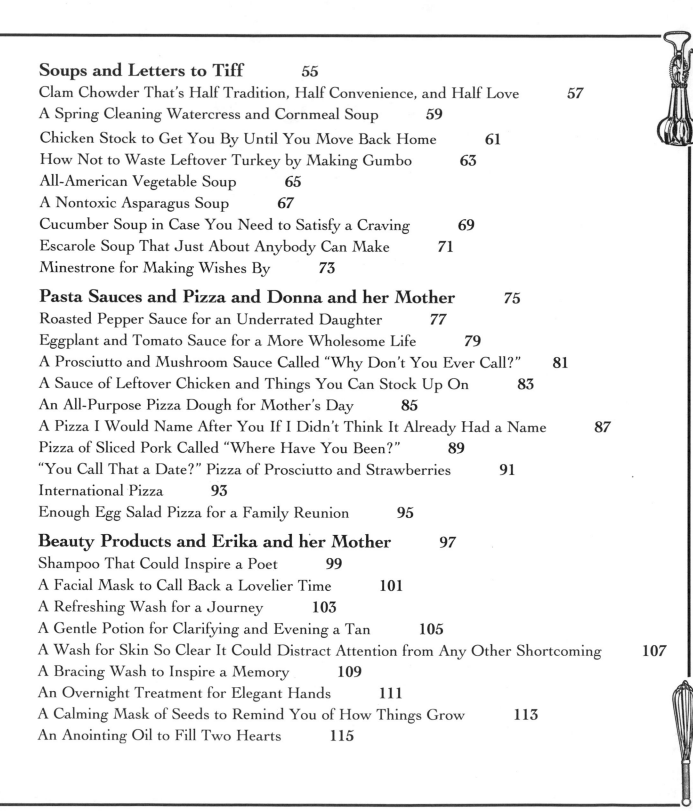

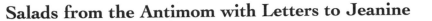

Acknowledgments

It is my good fortune that these pages won their appearance through the brilliant eyes and brilliant hands of Fran Lee and her talented associate Sean O'Neill. And no one better knows that the language is a living thing than Amy Teschner, who generously made this project the education I have always longed for. Laura Spargo bucked me up all the time, and threw off thrilling inspirations like it was easy. Thank you Jackie Hoffman, Jimmy Doyle, Alton Miller, Rose Abdoo, and Brian Quarles and Tom Bell. And Norman and Anthony and X.

Dear Reader,

While conducting scholarly research on the history and stunted development of the self-help genre, I stumbled upon these curious documents, apparently abandoned by their original collector. My colleagues insist that this portfolio was intentionally discarded, but the fact that these letters were found covered with food and coffee stains in a recycling bin is a clear indication that they were planted for my discovery. Within each mother and daughter exchange there is a profound and archetypal story, and, more important, there are recipes screaming to be prepared.

What follows, then, are original letters from mothers to daughters, with answers from daughters where they were available, printed as they were found, in the writer's own hand. The recipes have been reproduced for your convenience, as many were written on surfaces too disgusting to describe, encrusted with shards of oil, flour, and whatever. Believe me, this was a labor of love. As a mother might say, "I hope you're satisfied."

Margaret Sullivan

Not-So-Subliminal Messages

"Recipes are traditions, not just random wads of ingredients."
—Psychologist unknown

The recipes that follow have been tested in the field as well as the laboratory, and have been icon-coded for your enhanced understanding according to the interpreted philosophies of the mothers and their probable motivations in creating the recipes and choosing to communicate through them to their daughters, stepdaughters, or daughters-in-law.

affordable

gets you lots
of leftovers

lets you use
lots of kitchen gadgets

makes a perfect
hostess gift

helps you
find a husband

has fertility
drug potential

brings you
closer to nature

brings you
closer to Mom

Breads and Letters
to
Mary Catherine

*"Not one of them
is like another.
Don't ask me why
Go ask your mother."*
—**Dr. Seuss**

We begin with a lesson in the importance of incessant and redundant communication between mother and daughter. In his earliest work, *Personally Adequate and How!* Cornhusker explains the relationship between repetitive movements in food preparation, like kneading, and the need for verbal repetition in mother-daughter unions. See also, *Kneading and Needing* by the same author.

Another Beautiful Day . . .

Dear Mary Catherine,

Last time I was over when I was helping you out by dusting the inside of your closets and drawers, I happened to discover a little tape among your confusing belongings by some singers who call themselves The Jesus and Mary Chain.

I was so tickled to see you are going back to church again.

You've sure got the wardrobe for it. I only had one to see me through Senior Prom, Graduation and your Aunt Melanie's Cotillion. As you know, those party dresses.

Somehow I managed. I guess we all have to.

Love,
Mom

P.S. I'm not so sure I want to remind you with all of your crazy ideas, but don't forget to vote.

Enough Bran Muffins So There's Always Something Good to Eat

Before you start, be sure to set your oven temperature for 350.

2½ cups of raisin bran cereal, which you should always have around in case you suffer from irregularity

¼ cup butter

½ cup steamed milk

¾ cup brown sugar

1 egg

1½ cups flour

1 teaspoon soda

1 cup half and half

Juice of ½ lemon

A sprinkle of allspice

A sprinkle of cinnamon

Divide the raisin bran in half. If you had to share everything the way I did when I was young, this part will be easy. Half the raisin bran goes into a mixture of butter and the hot milk. Bring in the other ingredients as they appear above, and mix well. Then add in the remaining half of the cereal. Pour the batter into your adorable muffin cups and bake for one hour.

That will get you twelve muffins, but you'll probably only eat two. Then you'll toss the rest into the refrigerator to dry out over the days, until someone like your mother comes along to clear things away. You might dust them on top with a bit of flour so your plastic wrap doesn't stick.

Another Beautiful Day . . .

Dear Mary Catherine,

Well, I must speak one of those foreign languages or whatever because I'm pretty darn sure I asked at least a dozen times.

Will one of you girls please write your Uncle Marty a thank you note for the new fish tank and all the food and what have you? All it takes is a little thoughtful minute when you're not thinking about your clothes or some boy to sit down and write a little note.

I'm sure it won't put you in the poorhouse to buy a stamp or two.

Love,
Mom

Currant Scones as a Refresher Course in Good Manners

Be sure to set your oven temperature for 475 before you start.

1 cup flour
1½ teaspoons baking powder
½ teaspoon salt
1 teaspoon sugar
A dab of butter
¼ cup milk
1 egg
½ cup dried currants

Sift together all the dry ingredients, then cut in the butter and use the milk and egg to moisten the dough. Knead it delicately on a floured surface, then fold in the currants. Cut into triangle shapes and sprinkle with sugar. While you are baking this, you'll have all the time in the world to write a quick note to someone who might be waiting for one, which is ten minutes tops.

Another Beautiful Day . . .

Dear Mary Catherine,

Well, it's Easter next month, and I think you should start picking out your cards right away. People who wait until Good Friday get everybody's leftovers, you know.

Last year, you'll remember I had to send them out for you. Here's praying people don't know your handwriting, but who could? Who's seen it since you were in the third grade before you found out about boys when you used to have a spare second or two to think about somebody who might need to get a card for Easter.

Love,
Mom

Two Cheeses Bread Wreath to Celebrate a Holiday

Before you do anything, set your oven to 375 degrees.

1 envelope dry yeast
Water in amount recommended on the yeast
    package or ¾ cup
½ teaspoon salt
½ teaspoon baking soda
1 teaspoon sugar
Handful of caraway seeds
2½ cups flour
½ cup Romano cheese
½ cup Parmesan cheese
1 egg
Butter to baste the top
Ground black pepper

Dissolve the yeast in warm water and mix in everything but the butter and pepper. Work it up into a dough and knead for a while. If you can't say one whole rosary during this part, you haven't given it enough attention. Let it rise for a half hour in a covered bowl. Halve the dough and form into two wide strips that you can twist together. Then form a circle and meld the ends together. Let it rise another hour, then baste on melted butter and grind the pepper over the top. Bake for one half hour.

Another Beautiful Day . . .

Dear Mary Catherine,

Well, if you had called last night, you would know that your Dad and I were celebrating our first year in our new business.

It was a rocky start alright. I suppose I didn't expect the first year to be paved with rose petals. Aren't we pioneers, selling pump spray bottles of holy water? I thought your idea of "For home, car, office or boat" was really clever. But your Dad says you're just making fun of us again.

Sure would have been great to have gotten a little acknowledgement. Maybe a card or two from one of you girls.

Love,
Mom

Cinnamon Rolls to Acknowledge
an Accomplishment

You should set your oven temperature to 475 before you begin.

2 cups flour
½ cup butter
3 teaspoons baking powder
1 teaspoon salt
1 teaspoon cinnamon
2 beaten eggs
½ cup milk
2 tablespoons powdered sugar

*F*irst combine the flour and butter until it gets crumbly. Then add in the other dry ingredients. Work it into a dough with the eggs and milk to moisten. Roll it out a few extra times as a way of completing the kneading, but not too much, or they get heavy and tough. Don't expect any gratitude or acknowledgment from anybody, even though you're making these from scratch. You can cut these out with the open end of a water glass, and bake them on a greased sheet for ten minutes. You can glaze these while they're warm with a mixture of powdered sugar and a few drops of warm water.

Another Beautiful Day . . .

Dear Mary Catherine,

I'm blowing the whistle on you right now. You know there was no St. Buddy! And you had me driving to every library in the diocese trying to look him up.

You know your Dad and I don't want you going with a boy named Buddy. How could he possibly be Catholic?

In case you might like to know, I was just trying to find out this Saint's Day so I could send him a card. Some people like to show their feelings by sending a little card now and then.

Love,
Mom

Raspberry Bread for Saint Buddy's Day

Before you do anything, set your oven for 350.

2 eggs
½ cup olive oil
3 tablespoons white sugar
2 tablespoons brown sugar
1½ cups raspberries, which you will, of
   course, wash very carefully
1 teaspoon vanilla
1½ cups flour
½ teaspoon baking soda
½ teaspoon salt

*C*ombine the eggs, oil, and sugars thoroughly, then add the slightly mashed raspberries and vanilla. Sift together the other dry ingredients, then combine with the raspberry mixture. Maybe there's a Saint Norbud or Buddinger that Buddy is just a nickname for. Bake in a floured and greased loaf pan for one hour.

Another Beautiful Day . . .

Dear Mary Catherine,

I finally got a card from you and it's for one of those crazy art openings.

You know we think your special gifts are really interesting. I remember that nutty thing you did with the wallpaper pulled down and those weird Revelation quotes written all over the underside. Where do you get those ideas anyway? Have you got some sort of problem with religion?

I have to say that some of the music and art you're into is just plain spooky.

Dad says no way would you invite us if you thought we'd actually come. Well, maybe we'll surprise you.

Love,
Mom

Nutty Banana Bread for Your Nutty Art and Music

Before you do anything at all, be sure you preheat the oven to 350.

1 cup butter
1 teaspoon salt
2 cups sugar, that's right, that's a lot of sugar
4 eggs
4 cups flour
2 teaspoons baking soda
6 extra-ripe bananas, mashed
2 cups shelled walnuts

*C*ombine butter, salt, and sugar; then beat in eggs. Sift together the other dry ingredients, add in, and follow with the bananas and nuts. This will make four little loaf breads, which are baked in greased and floured pans for forty minutes. If you don't have loaf pans because you spent your money on makeup instead, you can make two cake pan-sized breads in about five minutes less time.

Another Beautiful Day . . .

Dear Mary Catherine,

Well it's not even Thanksgiving yet, and I've got all of my X-mas shopping out of the way. I've got your father done and Ethyl and George. I've got you done and all the nieces and cousins, the mailman, or do we say mail carrier nowadays? I've got all the girls in the altar society, the flower chairwoman, the linens captain; Father Pete and the new one.

But I've got one thread hanging, you know. I don't know what to get your young man. Does he even celebrate the birth of our Lord with a name like Buddy? I wonder. How about one of those cute caps with the sports teams on top, or a Dirt Devil. You let me know.

Love,
mom

Less Than 100 Days Till Christmas Bread

Be absolutely sure that you set your oven first for 400 degrees.

2 tablespoons butter
½ cup minced fruit, like apricots or apples
1 cup flour
¼ cup sugar
1 teaspoon baking powder
½ teaspoon salt
½ teaspoon cinnamon
½ teaspoon allspice
1 egg
¼ cup half-and-half

*C*ut the butter together with the minced fruit, then combine with the other ingredients. This will make two lovely little loaf cakes baked in greased and floured pans for thirty minutes. You could make a lot of these and use them as Xmas gifts for those scary people who park your car at work, or your strange chiropractor or whatever.

Another Beautiful Day . . .

Dear Mary Catherine,

After undoing your Dads hernia stitches driving over those bumpy railroad tracks, past that place where they tow your cars all stocked with mean Dobermans, down an alley full of hoodlum symbols painted everywhere, We finally found your gallery all covered in barbed wire.

None of that could have prepared us for the craziness we saw. "What was crazier and scarier," said your Dad, "the paintings or the so called performance piece?"

Next day I went straight to Father Pete and got you a counseling appointment. He's an expert, you know, on youthful despair. Don't say you can't get there because your Dad is taking the whole day off to pick you up and bring you back.

Love,
Mom

Bread That, with a Cup of Coffee, Can Remedy Youthful Despair

Don't start measuring anything until you have set your oven for 400.

½ cup sugar
¼ cup brown sugar
¼ cup butter
2 eggs
½ cup half-and-half
1½ cups flour
1½ teaspoons baking powder
½ teaspoon salt
3 teaspoons cinnamon

*M*ix together the sugars, butter, eggs, and cream. Sift the dry ingredients together and fold them in. This can be baked in a 9-inch round pan for a half hour. I think I read a study that showed that girls who bake lovely smelling things have an easier time meeting young people who don't necessarily have to flock to alienating industrial neighborhoods just to have a nice evening.

Dear Mary Catherine,

Well, you cancelled on Fr. Pete, and I guess I'm the fool for thinking you would go. Your Dad asked me this question last night, "They won't write letters, which is what you most want them to do, and they're into some weird pastimes, and Mary Catherine made you look stupid in front of Fr. Pete, but otherwise have they been good enough kids?"

I can't describe the fountain of memories that poured out as I thought that through, its to say nothing of feeling like an ingrate for being so mad at everybody all the time. I'm not saying I don't have every right. But I am remembering a summer night when I watched you sitting on top of the car in the driveway. The honeysuckle bush was hanging over the fence from that horrible Mr. Bell's house next door, and it sort of made a crown around your hair.

You were writing out your songs to send them to Lou Reed. I showed you how to get his address from the back of the record. Letter after letter, you just wanted to get his attention. The next day all the stamps were missing from the desk. You were only thirteen. You must have worked so hard.

Love,
Mom

Flourless Cornbread
for a Fascinating Daughter

Preheat your oven to 475 degrees.

    2 tablespoons olive oil
    3 cups cornmeal
    1 teaspoon salt
    2 cups boiling water
    ¾ cup milk
    2 teaspoons baking powder
    2 eggs, beaten until frothy

Work the oil through the cornmeal and salt, then pour the boiling water over that mixture. Then add in the milk, and cool this down for about a half hour. Add the baking powder and eggs last. Then bake in a greased loaf pan for thirty minutes. This is like you—it never fails to be unique and wonderful.

Scented Potions
and
Nicôle and Amber

"O holy Mother Earth, O air and sun,
behold me. I am wronged."
—Aeschylus

Breaking the circle of competitive hostility with beauty products. See my monograph entitled *The Philosophical Anthropology of How Your Mom Smells* for background.

Dear Amber,

Listen, I've had a vision. You were in my dream last night. We were strolling along a forgotten beach, you and I in total simpatico. You were bathed in a knowing, gentle indigo light. I felt I could know you as you really, really are. I was so happy.

What do you think that means? Is that bad? If you can't page me to talk it over, call my therapist and offer your input in a voice message. Not Marina, but Sten. I've been going to him on Thursdays for body work. I just know he's responsible for opening me up so that I can explore all the incredibly special issues I've been discovering lately. I'm so glad you introduced us.

Oh, about your earthly burden, no, I cannot lend you money to get your truck released from the pound. You see, I feel that if I contribute to those bad political energies, like city government ennui, than I shall realize more bad energy in return.

Yours in light, Nicole

An Herbal Potpourri for Meaningful Dreams

A dozen or so blossoms each of:
Sweet woodruff
Lavender flowers
Rosemary
Roses
Orange blossoms

½ cup chamomile tea
1 cut vanilla bean
1 tablespoon orrisroot

*B*undle your flowers together and hang upside down to dry for one half of a moon's cycle. If they are too small to tie together, lay them out on screens to dry. Store your blossoms in glass containers, because plastic isn't Nature's, and it devours the precious oils. Toss everything together and store for one full lunar cycle.

Tie a handful into a little handkerchief and hang it above your bed.

Dear Amber,

My "Find Your Own Reality" group potluck was last Wednesday. Everyone was expected to bring one healing dish that had recently provided a vision of rebirth.

It was especially important for mothers to be represented before the Spirit with their daughters.

Is it me? Where were you?

Yours in Light,
Nicole

A Breath of Welcoming Mint
for Your Doorway

A dozen or so flowers of each:
Roses
Marigolds
Rosemary

1 tablespoon allspice
3 tablespoons mint leaves
3 tablespoons cardamom
1 tablespoon bay leaves
2 tablespoons coriander
2 tablespoons orrisroot
12 drops oil of lime
12 drops oil of lemon

Dry your flowers in the usual way. When you combine the ingredients, crush the dried bay leaves and mint leaves to release their aromas. Drop in the oils last. Store this in an open glass jar near your doorway.

Dear Amber,

I don't wish to come out and say that I'm angry, although I guess I am holding inside some anger. I'm feeling it, in fact, in my fourth shakra, which is where I most need to feel unencumbered. I suppose I would have to acknowledge, and have you bear witness to the fact, that I'm feeling deep anger within.

Every single growth partner had her family around her for the Lost Jaguars Of Belize fund raiser. My truth finger is twitching wildly now, so I have confirmation from within that you have actually never considered those tiny things without their mothers slaughtered in the jungle by sick mercenary poachers. I offered to buy you a dress and shoes to match mine.

As you know, I have a broad landscape of history with abandonment, and you now have contributed to that. I thank all my guides that Sven was free after that lonely night.

Yours in light,
Nicole

An Amulet to Support You When You're Adrift in a Sea of Strangers

Dry your flowers and use a handful each:
Rose petals
Lavender flowers
Rosemary
Geranium leaves
Orange peel

Add 2 tablespoons each:
Orrisroot
Allspice
Cloves
Coriander

And 12 drops each:
Oil of jasmine
Oil of heliotrope

*I*n a little drawstring sack, combine a bit of this with your purest feelings. Don't be afraid to feel every one of them. Wear it when you're feeling vulnerable. I have mine on right now.

Dear Mother,

I am amazed you think I can worry about jaguars when my transportation has been possessed by the city and my wages are being garnished for failed student loans. I have, however, considered the plight of motherless things. It must be nice to float about in your swirly psychedelic world meaningful world. Honestly, it's hard for me to go to parties since Sven has stopped calling me. I feel a little lonely and a bit strange.

love, Amber

A Pillow of Fragrance to Carry Off Loneliness

1 handful of each of these, dried:
Rose petals
Lavender
Geranium leaves
Frankincense
Myrrh
Cut cinnamon sticks

2 tablespoons each:
Ground cloves
Allspice
Nutmeg
Ground coriander
Orrisroot

12 drops of each of these oils:
Rose
Vetiver
Musk
Sandalwood

Sew all of this in a little sack. I once met a midwife in the Rocky Mountains who used her antique camisoles as potpourri pillows. She just cut away the straps and sewed the bodice as a pillow. She lived all by herself in Monarch Pass.

Dear Amber,

I am really feeling your rage about the thing that happened with your money. I can see that you resent me for not having struggled in the same way that you have. It is not my mission to lord out such things. I struggle too.

Perhaps I am not as shackled to the Earth as are you. But that is a choice we all make.

You are young and nubile enough to find a man you can really grow with. I am here. My heart is open. It is now.

Nicole

A Potpourri for Drawing Stability
Out of Chaos

Dry your flowers and leaves in the regular
    way, and use a handful each:
Allspice
Coriander
Cloves
Orrisroot

Add 1 cut vanilla bean

And 6 drops of each of these oils:
Patchouli
Sandalwood
Musk
Rose

*T*ie this into a cheesecloth pouch and attach it to your bath faucet so that you draw your bath water through it. Allow the aromas to permeate the walls you have created that separate you from the goals you would like to materialize.

Dear Amber,

At this writing, I am bathed in a warm, searching light, imagining Sven's universally masculine hand on my receiving shoulders! I am sitting in my power spot, and I am able to speak the truth. He shouldn't have stolen my files and my New Age Consumer Mailing List (NACML). Where do you think he went? I know everybody in Boulder, and he's not there.

Incidentally, my WommnWarriors class spotted you on their Know Your Enemy field trip last Wednesday. You were dancing completely exposed for blue collar workers at the Can Cannery.

What is your life about? Who are you?

Love,
Mother

A Wintry Pillow to Cry Into

Dry your flowers and take a handful each:
Rosemary flowers
Mint leaves
Leaves of thyme

Add 2 tablespoons each:
Cloves
Allspice
Orrisroot

And 3 drops of each of these oils:
Rosemary
Cloves

*S*ew sachets of this onto your bed pillow and emote.

Dear Mother,
I am myself, and I will be
content when the people in my
life take their rightful places,
when the mother is really a
mother and the daughter I can be
a daughter.
love, Amber

Finding-Your-Place-in-Creation Creation

½ cup of each of these dried ingredients:
Pine needles
Rose petals
Juniper berries
Bay leaves
Orange blossoms
Rosemary

Add 2 tablespoons each:
Orrisroot
Cloves
Allspice

And 4 drops of musk oil

When I breathe this in I remember a picnic in the woods with a four-year-old daughter who wanted to show me the world as much as I wanted to show it to her.

Sandwiches and Letters

to

Jackie

"Who ran to help me when I fell,
And would some pretty story tell,
Or kiss the place to make it well.
My mother."

—Ann Taylor

The inherent structure of the sandwich has been acknowledged by self-help authors the world over as a perfect metaphor for the combined stresses of urban and material life.

Dear Jackie,

So you're in a movie! Your dream ever since you found out about that Spiked Lee character.

I'm not even going to ask what kind of sleazy nincompoop dance you had to do to get the part. You were so good in chemistry.

Thanks for the $5,000. We'll be going to the fancy fruit markets on 84th Street now. I was going to get that painful bridgework redone, but your sister needs something for Harold. He's trying, but you know.

Love,
Mom

When Pears Call for a
Celebration Sandwich

8 slices white bread (for 4 sandwiches)
½ cup butter
4 bosc pears like you can't get just anywhere
1 teaspoon cinnamon
1 teaspoon sugar

Get your oven ready to 375 degrees. If you want to be like your frivolous Aunt Ethyl, just cut the crust off the bread like it isn't even food. Butter the slices on all sides and lay four slices in a 9 by 12-inch baking pan. If you went through what I did, you could look at that pan and think of being smashed in one single bed with three sisters. Slice the pears thinly and make layers that go pears, sprinkle of sugar and cinnamon, pears, sprinkle of sugar and cinnamon—until there's nothing left. Then crumble the other four slices of bread on top, almost like a casserole. Give it ten minutes.

Dear Jackie,

Your sister tells me you're all embarrassed about how I saw you jogging along 58th Street and had you picked up by that well-groomed cab driver, who wasn't easy to find.

How about thanking me for spending my last $8 until the first of the month when I can't pay the cable company?

What are you doing out there just running around? Is a mother supposed to just believe that you'll get home from God knows where you wind up? Is a mother supposed to just sit there?

Mom

A Helping Hamburger

1 pound ground round, because anything
    else is a waste of money, and doesn't
    cook fast enough to get black on the out-
    side and juicy on the inside the way you
    like it
2 cloves of crushed garlic
Salt and ground black pepper to taste
Worcestershire sauce to brush on
Teriyaki sauce to brush on
Regular hamburger rolls from your own
    grocery (you don't have to go running all
    over to get some "special" kind)

Work the garlic, salt, and pepper into the meat, and form four patties. Brush these with the sauces, and broil them fast. My broiler takes five minutes.

Dear Jackie,

Just like we thought, your gay friends made us want to crawl under the table when you brought them over here for dinner. Yes, it's insulting when I buy mackerel for $11.99 and nobody eats because maybe they're wearing too many bracelets to pick up a fork.

Why not a nice, hot meal? A nice, hot meal and maybe they wouldn't think they were so gay. Maybe they're just hungry.

Mom

A Sandwich to Solve the Problem
of Leftover Mackerel

About 1 serving of mackerel (or some other
    expensive fish) that was broiled in butter
    and probably something else good, if I
    made it
½ lemon's worth of juice
A few stems watercress
Salt and ground white pepper to taste
Toasted slices of white bread

*J*ust pile it all (except the bread, of course) in the food processor until it's
what your unfriendly cousin Elaine calls a mousse, which I think of as something that goes in your hair. You just spread it over toast, and you're happy.

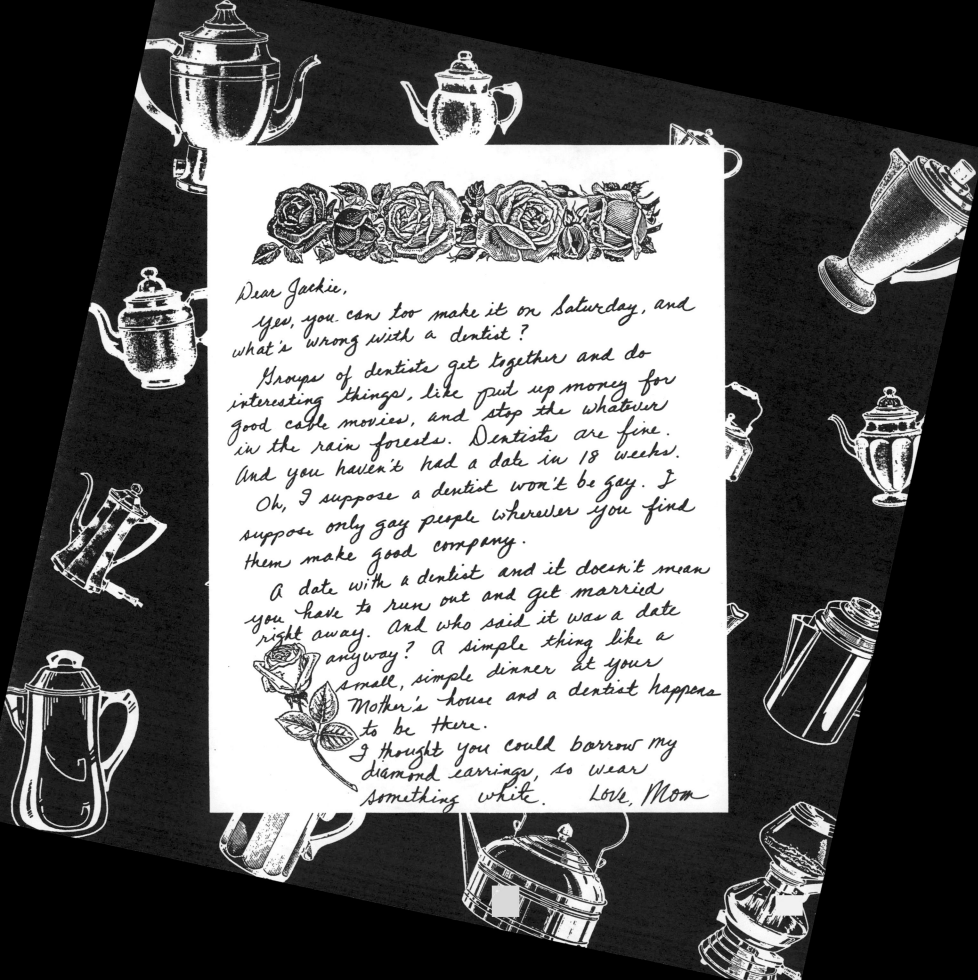

Dear Jackie,

Yes, you can too make it on Saturday, and what's wrong with a dentist?

Groups of dentists get together and do interesting things, like put up money for good cable movies, and stop the whatever in the rain forests. Dentists are fine. And you haven't had a date in 18 weeks.

Oh, I suppose a dentist won't be gay. I suppose only gay people wherever you find them make good company.

A date with a dentist and it doesn't mean you have to run out and get married right away. And who said it was a date anyway? A simple thing like a small, simple dinner at your Mother's house and a dentist happens to be there.

I thought you could borrow my diamond earrings, so wear something white.   Love, Mom

Make Sandwiches, Not Love

4 slices raisin bread (in case you're thinking of two)
Butter
4 slices Swiss cheese
1 apple, sliced

Roast your raisin bread and butter it. Get used to giving the man the more recent slices out of the toaster. Men like for things to be hot, and you should give them their way in the first three months. Make a bed of the Swiss cheese and apple slices, and top it off. Before you slice it, find out whether your companion likes his cut on the diagonal or horizontally.

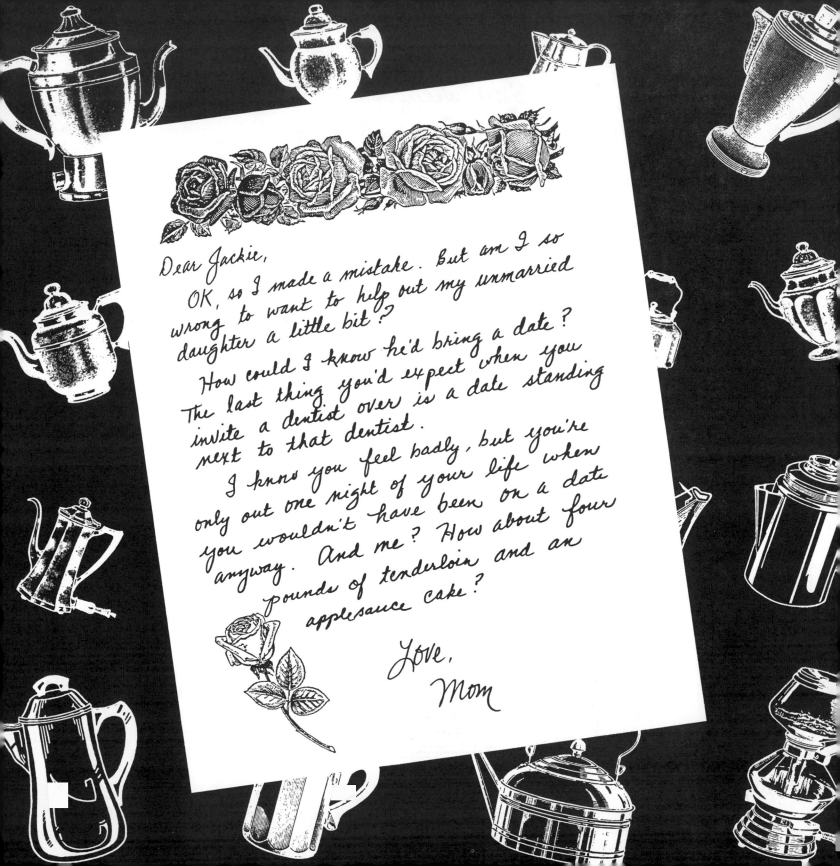

Dear Jackie,

OK, so I made a mistake. But am I so wrong to want to help out my unmarried daughter a little bit?

How could I know he'd bring a date? The last thing you'd expect when you invite a dentist over is a date standing next to that dentist.

I know you feel badly, but you're only out one night of your life when you wouldn't have been on a date anyway. And me? How about four pounds of tenderloin and an applesauce cake?

Love,
Mom

Post-Disappointment Roast Beef Sandwiches

½ cup butter
4 tablespoons flour
Sauce or pan drippings from the beef or
    ½ cup beef stock
Salt and ground black pepper to taste
Pinch of cloves
Slices of cold roast beef
Slices of black bread
Horseradish to spread

*B*rown the butter and flour over medium heat, stirring the whole time. Slowly add in your sauce (or stock) and flavorings. Lay in the beef slices and warm them up in the mixture. Transfer to the bread spread with horseradish, and serve with lots of pickles. This is Harold's favorite meal for after a job interview.

Dear Jackie,

Your sister tells me you're all embarrassed about me getting a job at the video store. I guess having your Mom out there working for $5.35 an hour is embarrassing for a movie actress.

Maybe I should try to get a big acting job as a crabby old lady in a carpet cleaning commercial and you could be real proud of me.

I think it's nice that I can get your cousin Sheila piano lessons, even though she doesn't ever say thank you. And all of my favorite movies are in the damage bin for free.

Love
Mom

Movie Night Cucumber Sandwiches

1 6-ounce block cream cheese
1 cucumber, minced
2 tablespoons olive oil
2 tablespoons vinegar
Juice of ½ lemon
Black pepper and salt to taste
Garnish of dill weed
Bagels

*M*ash everything except the bagels together with a fork until it's smooth enough to spread. You do need bagels for this, onion are best, because bread can't stand up to it. If you serve these with some deli meats on the side, then just about anybody can nibble on something; even a skinny vegetarian could be watching a movie and still have a little something.

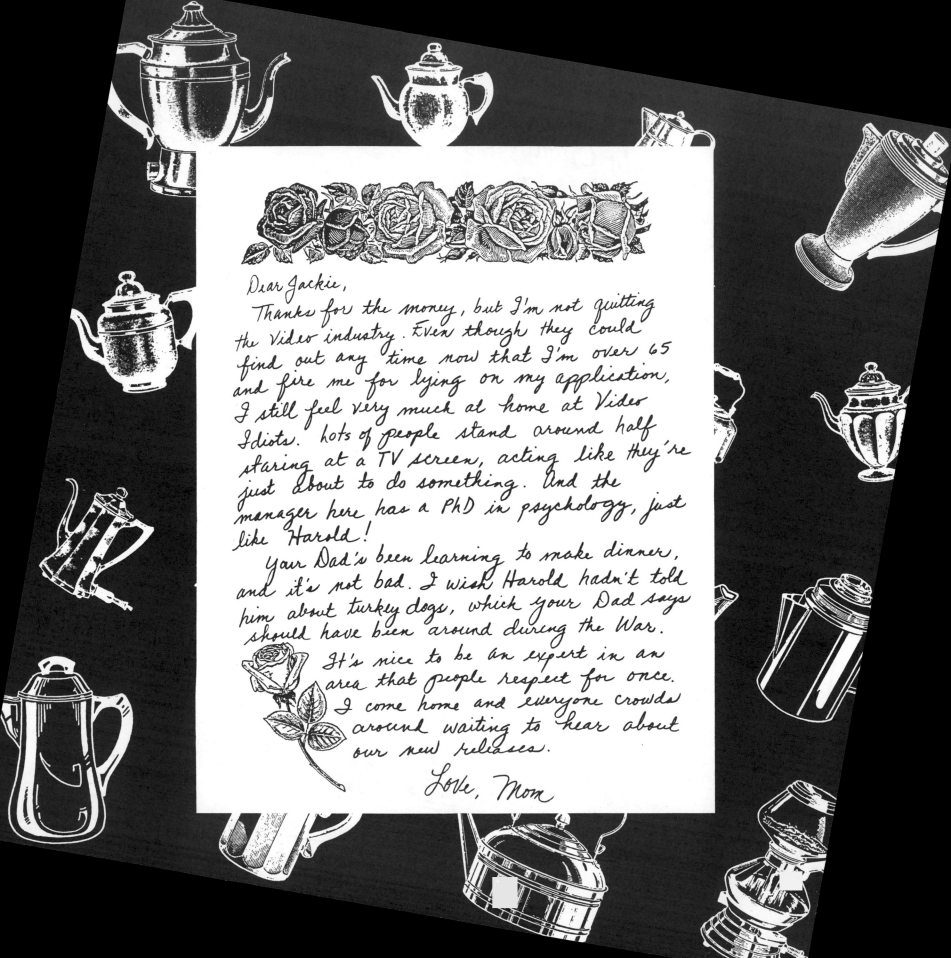

Dear Jackie,

Thanks for the money, but I'm not quitting the Video industry. Even though they could find out any time now that I'm over 65 and fire me for lying on my application, I still feel very much at home at Video Idiots. Lots of people stand around half staring at a TV screen, acting like they're just about to do something. And the manager here has a PhD in psychology, just like Harold!

Your Dad's been learning to make dinner, and it's not bad. I wish Harold hadn't told him about turkey dogs, which your Dad says should have been around during the War.

It's nice to be an expert in an area that people respect for once. I come home and everyone crowds around waiting to hear about our new releases.

Love, Mom

Home and Hearth Pastrami Sandwiches

Dark mustard
Coriander to taste
Slices of rye bread
Cream cheese to spread
Slices of pastrami

Spread the mustard and sprinkle coriander on half the slices of rye, and spread cream cheese on the others. Then pile on the pastrami. You know, everyone likes it differently. Your Dad likes a big pile in the middle of the bread, which is not at all like the way you like an even amount to touch all edges. Your sister likes it to look like it was just photographed by a magazine, but then she hardly takes a bite.

Dear Jackie,

Your sister probably ran to the phone the minute she heard this to tell you, but I am temporarily on probation from the video store for a simple little transgression.

It's gotten so I can tell the minute they walk in the door who's going to go back into the ADULT section, which, by the way, they keep unbelievably close to Family World.

So I quietly yelled, "Smut, smut, smut" to somebody who was, believe me, asking for it. It was the least I could do for all of society.

It's men like that who make it impossible for girls like you to meet men who aren't like that.

Love,
Mom

Defending the Universe with Feta Cheese Sandwiches

6 ounces feta cheese
A clove of crushed garlic
Black pepper and salt to taste
Italian bread
Olive oil to brush on
Basil leaves
½ red onion, minced

*G*et the cheese, garlic, and onions together in a bowl and mash with a fork until well blended. Then season. Toast slices of Italian bread, and brush with oil. Lay basil leaves on the bread slices before spreading with cheese, and enjoy.

Soups and Letters
to
Tiff

"Everything looks good tonight."
—Iggy Pop

*I*t has been recently discovered that the inclination to make soup is developmentally linked to the urge to find your spiritual home. And soup has long been accepted as a remedy for obsessive behavior.

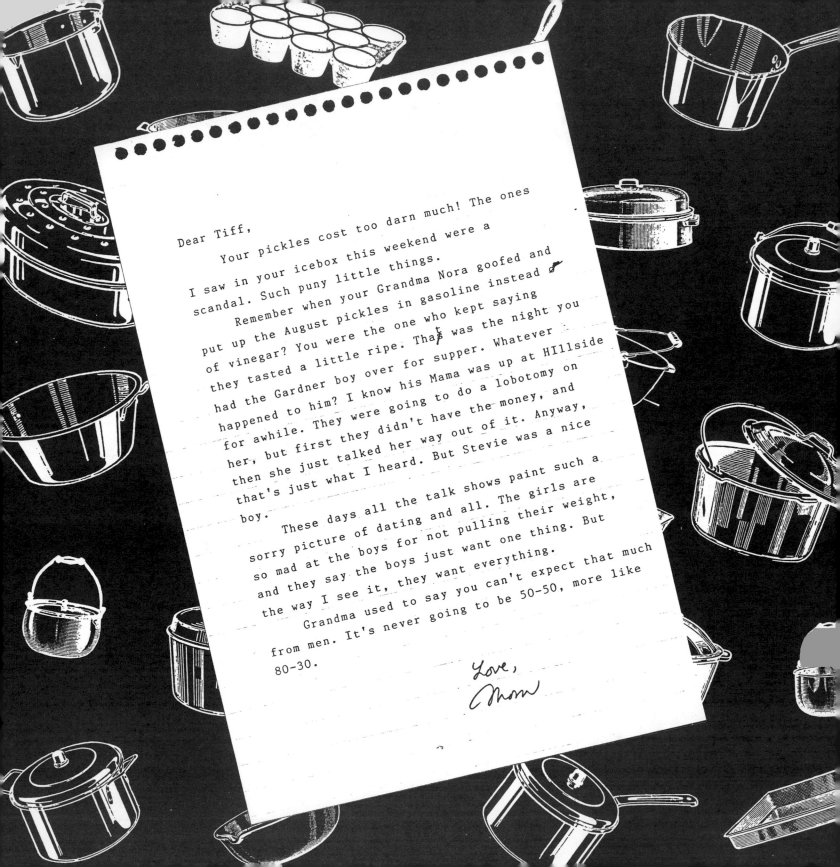

Dear Tiff,

Your pickles cost too darn much! The ones I saw in your icebox this weekend were a scandal. Such puny little things.

Remember when your Grandma Nora goofed and put up the August pickles in gasoline instead of vinegar? You were the one who kept saying they tasted a little ripe. That was the night you had the Gardner boy over for supper. Whatever happened to him? I know his Mama was up at HIllside for awhile. They were going to do a lobotomy on her, but first they didn't have the money, and then she just talked her way out of it. Anyway, that's just what I heard. But Stevie was a nice boy.

These days all the talk shows paint such a sorry picture of dating and all. The girls are so mad at the boys for not pulling their weight, and they say the boys just want one thing. But the way I see it, they want everything. Grandma used to say you can't expect that much from men. It's never going to be 50-50, more like 80-30.

Love,
Mom

Clam Chowder That's Half Tradition, Half Convenience, and Half Love

Have everything in front of you and ready to use before you begin.

1 small pail (the size of a sand castle–making
   pail) full of clams
2 strips bacon
1 tablespoon flour
½ white onion, chopped
4 red potatoes, chopped
3½ cups water
Salt and black pepper to taste
1 cup milk

Well, this is man's work (hint, hint), but you want to scrub those little devils in warm water. Then steam them in ½ cup water until they open up. That juice they've been steaming in is nothing to throw a stick at, so you'll want to send it along into the soup with the clam meats.

Fry your bacon until crisp, then set aside to drain. Add the flour to the warm grease to make a brown sauce. Then add in chopped onion to fry in that until brown. Now bring in the chopped potatoes, 3 cups of water, salt, and pepper. Cook all this for a half hour or so. Then add in the milk and clams for another ten minutes. You can thicken this with more flour, if you like, but be careful that you don't get it so thick that it looks like those soups they serve in lunchrooms that are attached to dime stores.

Dear Tiff,

It's nice you're cleaning out your closet for Spring. Don't get rid of things you might want later, though. I always use these rules:

Keep at least one thing from each of your relatives.

Don't get rid of anything that can be sold in one of those second-time-around places.

If you make donations, drive to another town, so you don't see your neighbors wearing yours castaways.

Never give away anything I gave you.

Give me a call if you want some help. I'd love to, you know.

Love,
Mom

A Spring Cleaning Watercress and Cornmeal Soup

I always like to make sure I have everything out in front of me before I start.

3 tablespoons butter or the same amount of
   olive oil
1 clove of garlic, crushed
1 bunch watercress
2 quarts chicken broth
Salt and ground black pepper to taste
1 cup cornmeal

Melt the butter or heat the oil with the garlic and add the rinsed watercress. It's fine if a bit of water clings to the leaves. Cook gently four or five minutes, then transfer it to a food processor or blender and puree for just a second, or chop it finely. Now back it goes to the pot with the chicken broth, salt, and pepper. Let this heat for thirty minutes or so. Every once in a while sift a portion of the cornmeal into the cooking soup and stir it until smooth. If it stays lumpy, thin the cornmeal out with flour sifted through it. This is a delicious way to get rid of that last cup of cornmeal sitting around. But don't throw out the box if it's like the ones oatmeal comes in. Kids in your neighborhood may be making pinhole cameras or homemade trains. You never know when someone will come to your door and ask for one, and you don't want to be one of those people who has to say no.

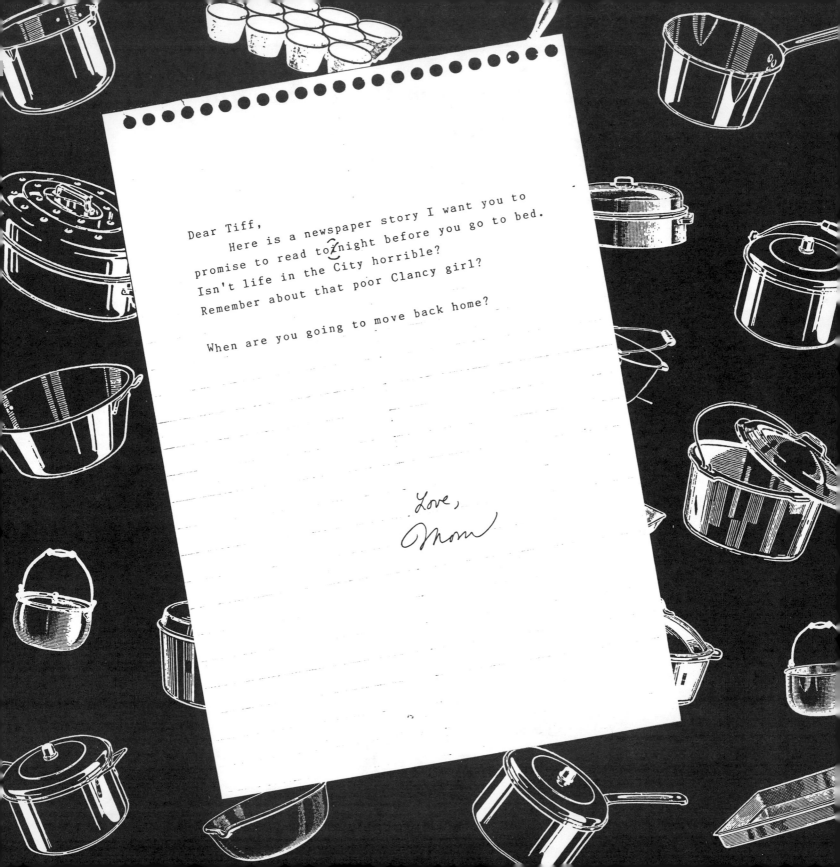

Dear Tiff,
            Here is a newspaper story I want you to
promise to read tonight before you go to bed.
Isn't life in the City horrible?
Remember about that poor Clancy girl?

When are you going to move back home?

                Love,
                Mom

Chicken Stock to Get You By Until You Move Back Home

How about getting all your things ready before you start?

You'll need a chicken, a whole 2-pound one
    or a mostly eaten larger one
1 gallon water, which will boil down to 2 or
    3 quarts
3 carrots
3 stalks celery
1 white onion
Salt and ground white pepper to taste

Keep your stock clear and simple because you'll want to use it for a lot of different things. Chop your vegetables and combine them with everything else in a big pot over medium heat for at least two hours covered and one hour not covered. Every now and then clear away the fat that rises. There are as many ways to do that as you've got second cousins. I like to fill a colander with ice and strain it through that twice before I store it because the fat seems to like the cold and gets gathered up around it. Then you store it in the refrigerator to use for all the soups you're going to want to make. Or one night, when you're really hungry, you can make rice with it and think it's a real feast.

How Not to Waste Leftover Turkey
by Making Gumbo

Get all of these things together beforehand, so you don't go running around with your head cut off when you need them all of a sudden.

4 tablespoons flour
4 tablespoons butter
Ground white, red, and black pepper to taste
½ large bermuda onion, chopped
3 or 4 stems celery, chopped
2 cloves garlic, crushed
Good pieces leftover turkey
All the seafood you can get, especially
    shrimp, oysters, and crabs to equal at
    least 1 pound
3 tablespoons gumbo filé

*M*ake a gravy of the flour, butter, and pepper, and fry everything but the seafood and filé in that. I know you won't because you're such a lady, but don't use that kind of turkey that comes in a bag like Mrs. Zulevic does or people will talk. You know, that kind that's in the refrigerator case with the cheese that's already shredded. Don't get that. Then you can pour on the water, add the seafood, and just wait. Keep the whole thing on medium low for two hours, and add your gumbo filé in the last five minutes. Now, I hope that's not all you're having for dinner. You need a salad and at least one side, like rice would be perfect.

Dear Tiff,

It's just a shame that your company is making you go to Rome this Spring. It seems like every time things start to go well for you, you get sidetracked. I guess you'll have to stay in some cramped little hotel room. And you'd better bring along shoes you can walk in. They can't possibly have the convenient transportation we have here.

Love,
Mom

All-American Vegetable Soup

It helps to have everything out and ready before you start.

3 carrots
1 turnip
3 stalks celery
3 red potatoes
2 handfuls of green beans
½ white onion
4 tablespoons butter
4 tablespoons flour
Salt to taste
Parsley to make it pretty

*C*hop all your vegetables and set them over a medium flame in a pot with about 1 gallon of water. When I say all your vegetables I mean all but the onion. That you fry in the brown sauce that you make with the butter and flour. When that's all just brown and smelling good, you add it to the simmering water and vegetables. Then you continue cooking two hours, adding the parsley in the last five minutes.

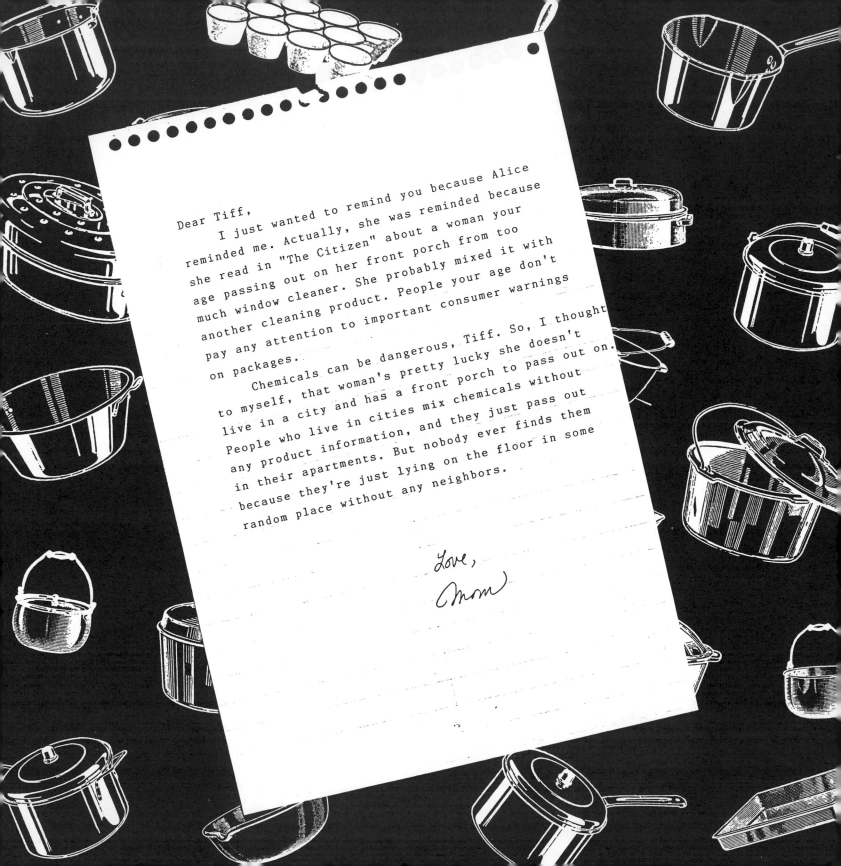

Dear Tiff,

I just wanted to remind you because Alice reminded me. Actually, she was reminded because she read in "The Citizen" about a woman your age passing out on her front porch from too much window cleaner. She probably mixed it with another cleaning product. People your age don't pay any attention to important consumer warnings on packages.

Chemicals can be dangerous, Tiff. So, I thought to myself, that woman's pretty lucky she doesn't live in a city and has a front porch to pass out on. People who live in cities mix chemicals without any product information, and they just pass out in their apartments. But nobody ever finds them because they're just lying on the floor in some random place without any neighbors.

Love,
Mom

A Nontoxic Asparagus Soup

Why not get everything out and in reach before you begin?

3 tablespoons butter
3 tablespoons flour
Salt and white pepper to taste
6 to 8 spears of leftover cooked asparagus
   or new asparagus steamed for five minutes
2 cups chicken stock
2 cups milk or cream

*B*rown your butter and flour, then season it. Add in chopped cooked asparagus and continue to fry gently a few more minutes. Pour in your chicken stock and cook for thirty minutes, then add in milk or cream for another ten minutes. Try not to let this boil. Your Aunt Julia cooks this double-boiler style, but she's such a priss, always doing everything just so.

Cucumber Soup in Case You Need to Satisfy a Craving

Have these things out and ready to go.

2 cucumbers
2 tablespoons butter
1 quart chicken stock
½ cup milk or cream
Salt and black pepper to taste
Fresh dill weed for garnish

Puree your "cukes" after removing the seedy part and fry them in the butter on a low flame for about five minutes. Then pour in the stock and cook thirty minutes. Add the milk or cream and cook another five minutes without boiling. Salt and pepper to taste. Sprinkle the dill over each serving.

Penzione
Sergio Leone
ROMA

Tiff,

Gosh, if you like Italian food, Rome
sure is the place for it! I'm still
pinching myself because I think I must
be dreaming. My wobbly little colt
of a daughter has brought me on a
big business trip.

Did you ever imagine that men could
smell so good?

Love,
Mom

Escarole Soup That Just About Anybody Can Make

3 quarts chicken broth
Great big head of escarole lettuce, finely chopped
Splash of olive oil
Spaghetti that would fit inside a ring that you
    make of your baby finger and your thumb
3 tablespoons Parmesan cheese that you
    grate yourself
Ground black pepper to taste

Get the broth into a boil and add in the escarole, then boil gently for 20 minutes or so. You'd better cover it or you'll reduce your stock. Sprinkle in the oil before you add the pasta, then let that cook, but not too long. They don't like their pasta all mushy like it's been in a can, you know. I wish you could get one of those handsome, handsome boys with the big puppy dog eyes to grate your cheese over the soup like I've been having. Then, have him come back with the pepper grinder.

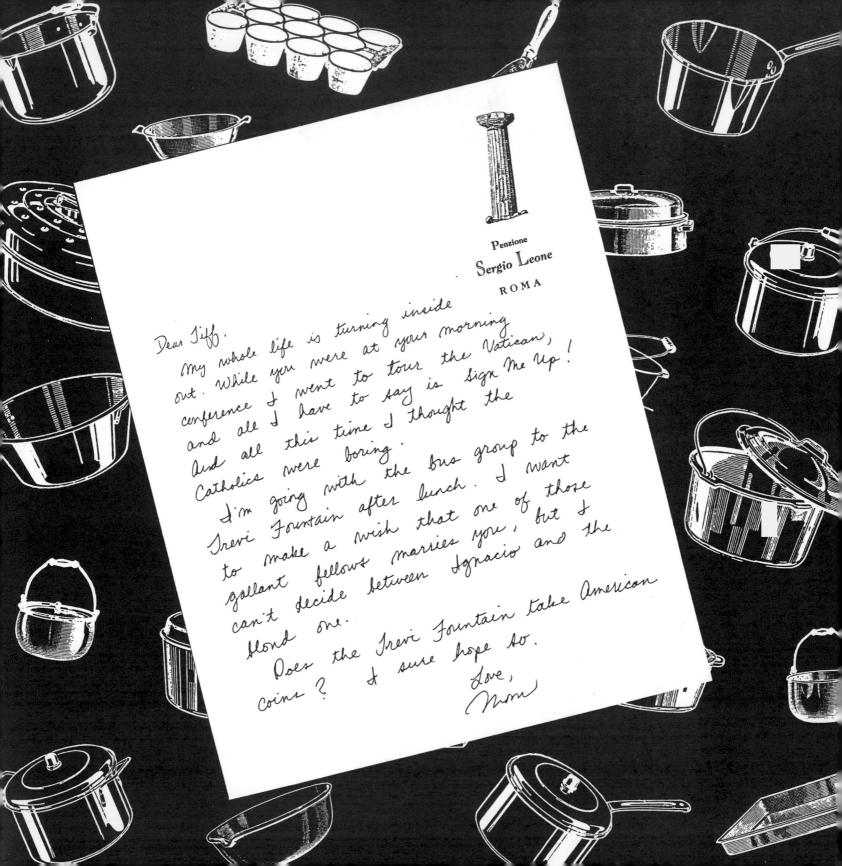

Penzione
Sergio Leone
ROMA

Dear Tiff,

My whole life is turning inside out. While you were at your morning conference I went to tour the Vatican, and all I have to say is sign me up! And all this time I thought the Catholics were boring.

I'm going with the bus group to the Trevi Fountain after lunch. I want to make a wish that one of those gallant fellows marries you, but I can't decide between Ignacio and the blond one.

Does the Trevi Fountain take American coins? I sure hope so.

Love,
Mom

Minestrone for Making Wishes By

3 carrots
3 stalks celery
½ white onion
1 ripe tomato
3 white potatoes
1 zucchini
4 strips bacon
1 cup white beans that should be soaked
    the night before
1 cup macaroni
Salt and ground black pepper to taste
Handful chopped parsley
Grated Parmesan

*C*hop the carrots, celery, onion, tomato, potatoes, and zucchini. Fry your bacon until it's almost crisp, then add in your carrots, celery, onion, and tomato. Send all this to a bigger pot, and pour three pints of water over it. When it boils, you can add the potatoes and beans. After an hour, you can add the zucchini and pasta and cook another five minutes. Just before serving, salt and pepper to taste and add the parsley. Sprinkle with your grated Parmesan when you serve. As you know, I bought seven of those shiny metal cheese graters with the crank handles. It looks like everybody I know is getting one for Christmas!

Pasta Sauces and Pizza
and
Donna and her Mother

"Mother, give me the sun."
—Henrik Ibsen

We learn that love is psychologically equivalent to neurotic concern, and that love of a mother's tomato sauce is equivalent to love of a mother.

The Bryants

Dear Donna,

I've got one hand on my laptop and one on the telephone, and you know who's going to get a call from me! Who does that Mr. Florence think he is, giving the promotion to that condescending redhead who treats me like dirt on the phone? I could spit.

What kind of a first name is Florence? He's got ghosts in the attic alright.

Does he have the slightest idea how well you did in school? Does he know you studied Russian, of all things? Now, have you ever sent him your transcripts? I'll bet you never have. Well, at least I can do that for you. I've got to do something.

I suppose you'll get all embarrassed if I call him again. Don't want your mom calling your Boss, I suppose.

After all, I'm just

Your Mom

Roasted Pepper Sauce for an Underrated Daughter

Buy your groceries on Mondays or Thursdays, because that's when new things come in.

½ pound bacon
1 white onion, minced
2 cloves garlic, crushed
6 anchovies
4 to 6 tomatoes
1 or 2 red peppers
2 tablespoons olive oil

*F*ry the bacon until nearly crisp, then fry the minced onion and garlic in the same pan until the bacon has become crispy and the onion is transparent. Then bring in the anchovies and cook for another five minutes on a lower flame. Blanch the tomatoes so you can peel them more easily, then remove the seeds and dice them. Trim your peppers and remove the seeds and membrane and dice. Toss the tomatoes and peppers in oil before adding them to the pan. Does Mr. Florence know what a brilliant cook you are? I guess you'll say he doesn't care. Then cook about fifteen minutes on a low flame. You can start your pasta now. I'm thinking rotini.

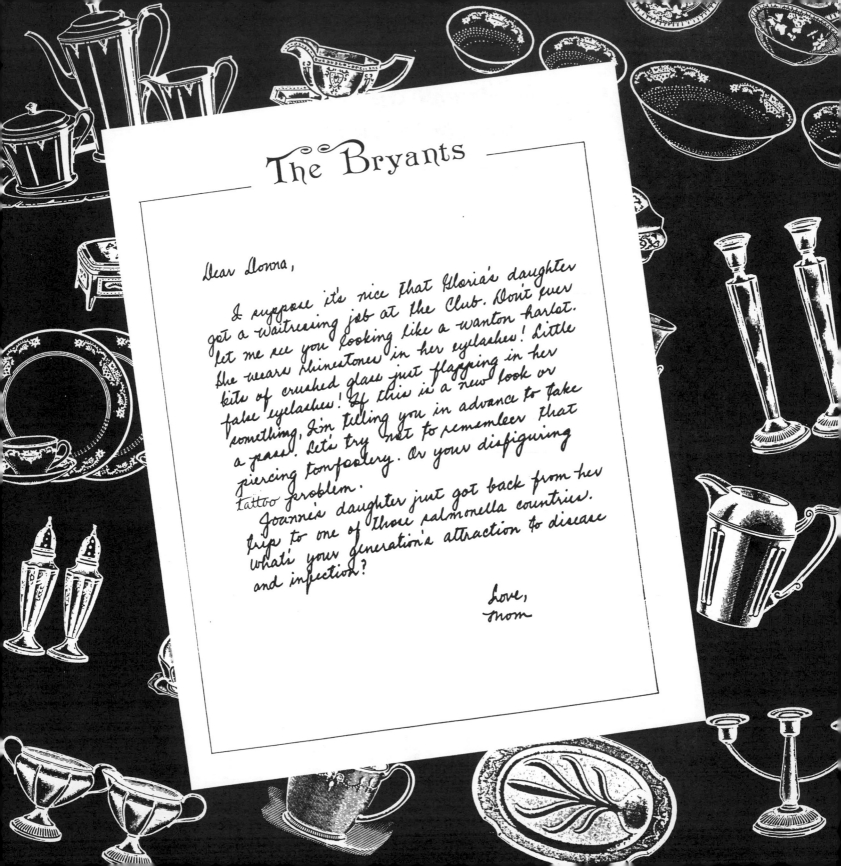

The Bryants

Dear Donna,

I suppose it's nice that Gloria's daughter got a waitressing job at the Club. Don't ever let me see you looking like a wanton harlot. She wears rhinestones in her eyelashes! Little bits of crushed glass just flapping in her false eyelashes! If this is a new look or something, I'm telling you in advance to take a pass. Let's try not to remember that piercing tomfoolery. Or your disfiguring tattoo problem.

Joanne's daughter just got back from her trip to one of those salmonella countries. What's your generation's attraction to disease and infection?

Love,
mom

Eggplant and Tomato Sauce for a More Wholesome Life

It's best to go to the vegetable market on Thursdays or Mondays when things are fresh.

1 eggplant
1 yellow pepper, seeded and sliced
4 tablespoons olive oil
1 clove garlic, crushed
4 tomatoes, peeled, seeded, and minced
4 anchovies
A dozen or so pitted black olives
The same amount of capers
Basil for garnish

I hate to put it this way, but you've got to "sweat" your eggplant. Slice thin and lay the slices on paper towels; then cover them with a layer of paper towels. Put an even weight on them, like that elegant coffee table book we gave you, I think it's called *All the Art All the Time*, and leave it a half hour. This will press out all the bitterness. While this is happening, be broiling the yellow pepper slices on a baking sheet just under the flame. Brown the eggplant in oil and garlic, then add the tomatoes. Five minutes later, add the broiled pepper slices, and five minutes after that, add in the anchovies, olives, and capers, and cook another five minutes. Your pasta should be extra thin for this, like spaghettini or capellini.

Donna,
Are you alive?
I was just curious.
It would be
interesting to know.
                                mom

KUNSTHISTORISCHES MUSEUM, WIEN
RAFFAELLO SANTI (1484–1520)
Die Madonna im Grünen, 1506
The Virgin in the Meadow
La Vièrge dans la Prairie

Shemps Temps
10 Vassar Avenue
Philadelphia, PA 19020
Attn: Donna Bryant
            U.S.A.

KHM 220

ČESKÁ REPUBLIKA
UNESCO

A Prosciutto and Mushroom Sauce Called "Why Don't You Ever Call?"

A dozen or so mushrooms, brushed off and quartered
3 tablespoons olive oil
1 clove garlic, crushed
½ pound prosciutto, torn into little pieces
2 tomatoes, blanched, seeded, peeled, and minced
1 teaspoon ground sage
1 teaspoon ground nutmeg
White pepper to taste
½ cup cream

*F*ry the mushrooms in the oil and garlic until caramelized. How are we supposed to have a good time when we don't even know if our kids are alive or dead? Were you just trying to destroy the one vacation we've taken in seven years? Bring in prosciutto and tomatoes and cook five minutes. Add in the sage, nutmeg, pepper, and cream last and cook another two or three minutes. Use this sauce with something broad like fettucine.

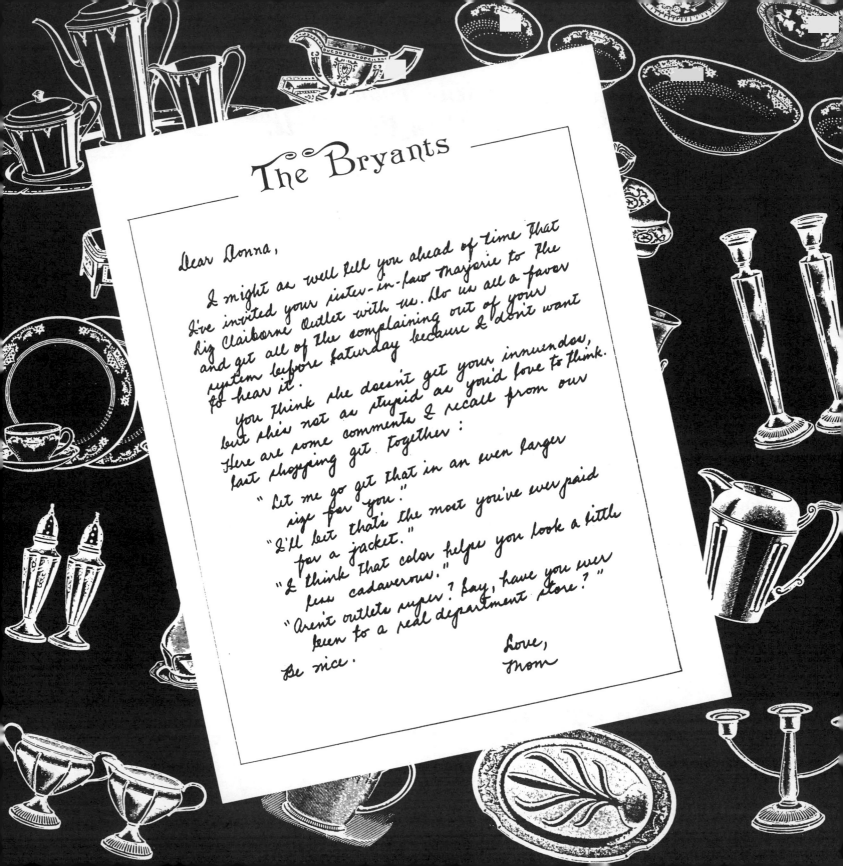

The Bryants

Dear Donna,

I might as well tell you ahead of time that I've invited your sister-in-law Marjorie to the Liz Claiborne Outlet with us. Do us all a favor and get all of the complaining out of your system before Saturday because I don't want to hear it.

You think she doesn't get your innuendos, but she's not as stupid as you'd love to think. Here are some comments I recall from our last shopping get together:

"Let me go get that in an even larger size for you."

"I'll bet that's the most you've ever paid for a jacket."

"I think that color helps you look a little less cadaverous."

"Aren't outlets super? Say, have you ever been to a real department store?"

Be nice.

Love,
Mom

A Sauce of Leftover Chicken and Things You Can Stock Up On

When you visit those warehouses, you can shop pretty much any day.

A dozen or so mushrooms, brushed off and
   quartered
2 tablespoons olive oil
2 tablespoons butter
1 clove garlic, crushed
About 1 pound of leftover chicken or capon, sliced
1 teaspoon cinnamon
Ground white pepper to taste
1 glass Marsala

*B*rown the mushrooms in the oil, butter, and garlic; then bring in the chicken and season with cinnamon and pepper. Cook for five minutes before you introduce the Marsala, then cook another ten minutes. I like this with linguine after a hard day of shopping.

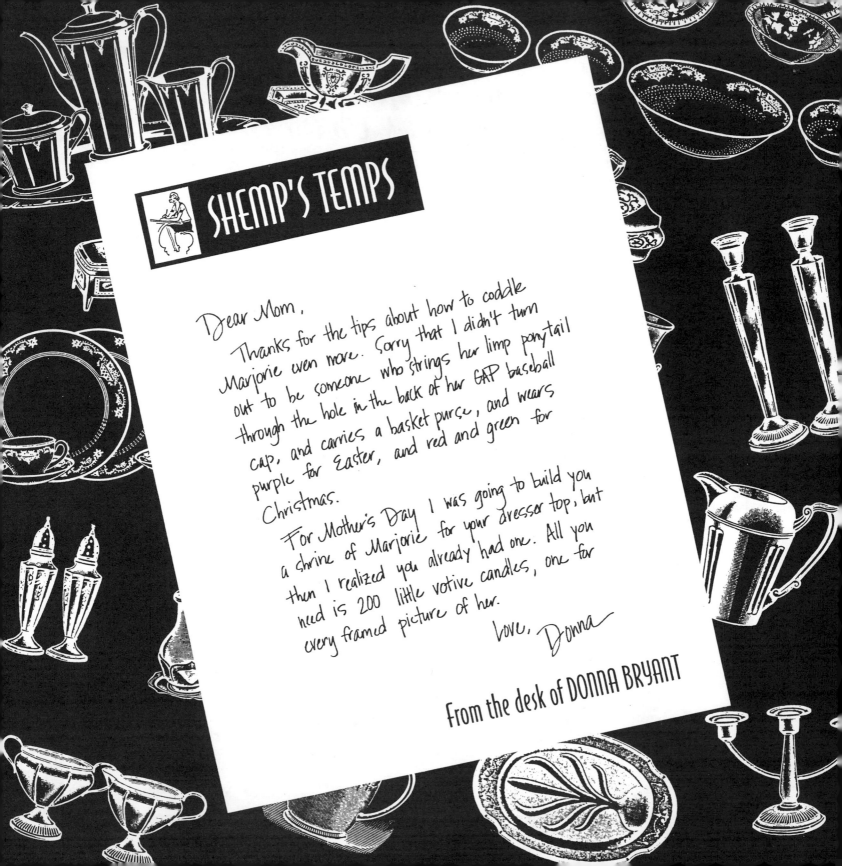

SHEMP'S TEMPS

Dear Mom,

Thanks for the tips about how to coddle Marjorie even more. Sorry that I didn't turn out to be someone who strings her limp ponytail through the hole in the back of her GAP baseball cap, and carries a basket purse, and wears purple for Easter, and red and green for Christmas.

For Mother's Day I was going to build you a shrine of Marjorie for your dresser top, but then I realized you already had one. All you need is 200 little votive candles, one for every framed picture of her.

Love, Donna

From the desk of DONNA BRYANT

An All-Purpose Pizza Dough
for Mother's Day

I guess it doesn't much matter when you buy flour and salt, as long as you don't have to do it on Mother's Day.

- 1 to 1½ cups water at bath temperature
- 1 teaspoon sugar
- 1 teaspoon dried yeast
- 2 cups flour
- ½ cup cornmeal
- 1 teaspoon salt
- 1 tablespoon olive oil

Add a little of the warm water to the sugar and yeast, and let it express itself, the way you say you never got to. It will get foamy when it's ready. Meanwhile, sift your flour, cornmeal, and salt together. When the yeast water is ready, combine everything, and knead thoroughly; ten minutes is good. Leave it covered for an hour to rise. Then you knead it again. Some Mother's Day, huh? At this point, all the handling you do is just for fun. You could be glamorous with it like your Dad and twirl it over your head, but I just move it into a 12-inch round and place it on a pizza pan greased with the olive oil. Bake according to the pizza recipe you are using.

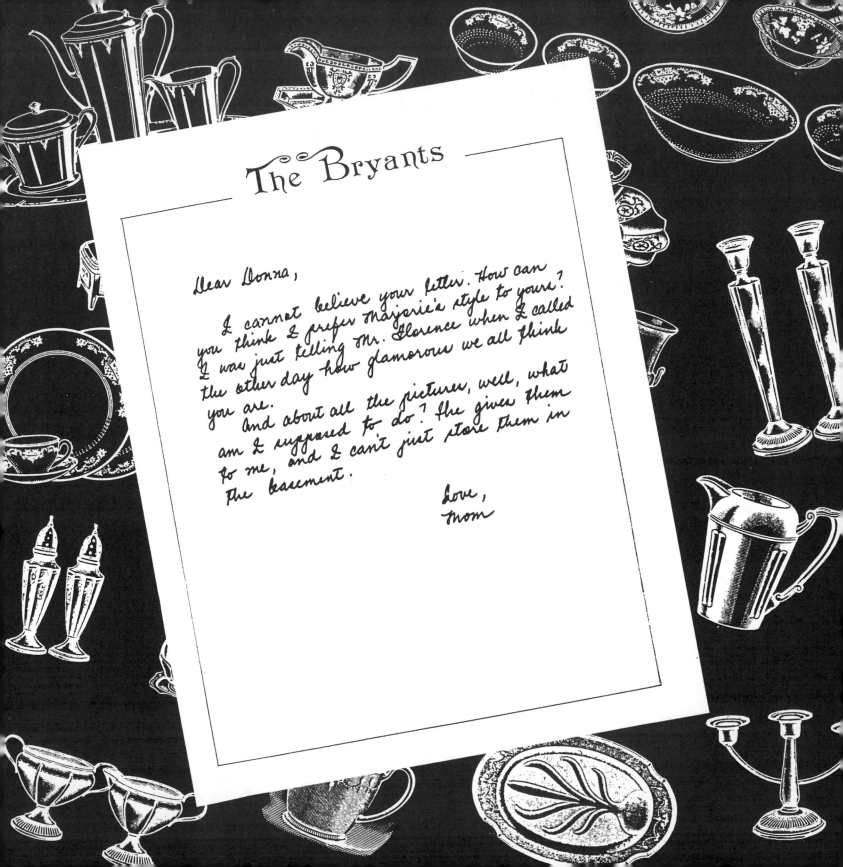

The Bryants

Dear Donna,

I cannot believe your letter. How can you think I prefer Marjorie's style to yours? I was just telling Mr. Florence when I called the other day how glamorous we all think you are.

And about all the pictures, well, what am I supposed to do? She gives them to me, and I can't just store them in the basement.

Love,
Mom

A Pizza I Would Name After You If I Didn't Think It Already Had a Name

Don't buy tomatoes from just anybody.

All-Purpose Pizza Dough for Mother's Day
   (see page 85)
4 tomatoes, blanched, peeled, seeded, and minced
1 white onion, minced
1 clove garlic, crushed
¼ cup olive oil
12 thin slices mozzarella
12 leaves of basil
Ground white and black pepper to taste

Start your oven at 450 degrees.
Make the sauce by frying your tomatoes, onions, and garlic in most of the oil. (Save a bit of the oil to sprinkle across your dough before you apply the sauce.) When the onions are transparent, the sauce is ready. Spread the rest of the olive oil on the dough and then spread the sauce on top of it. Next apply the slices of mozzarella and basil in an artful fashion, as only you would know. Bake for fifteen minutes.

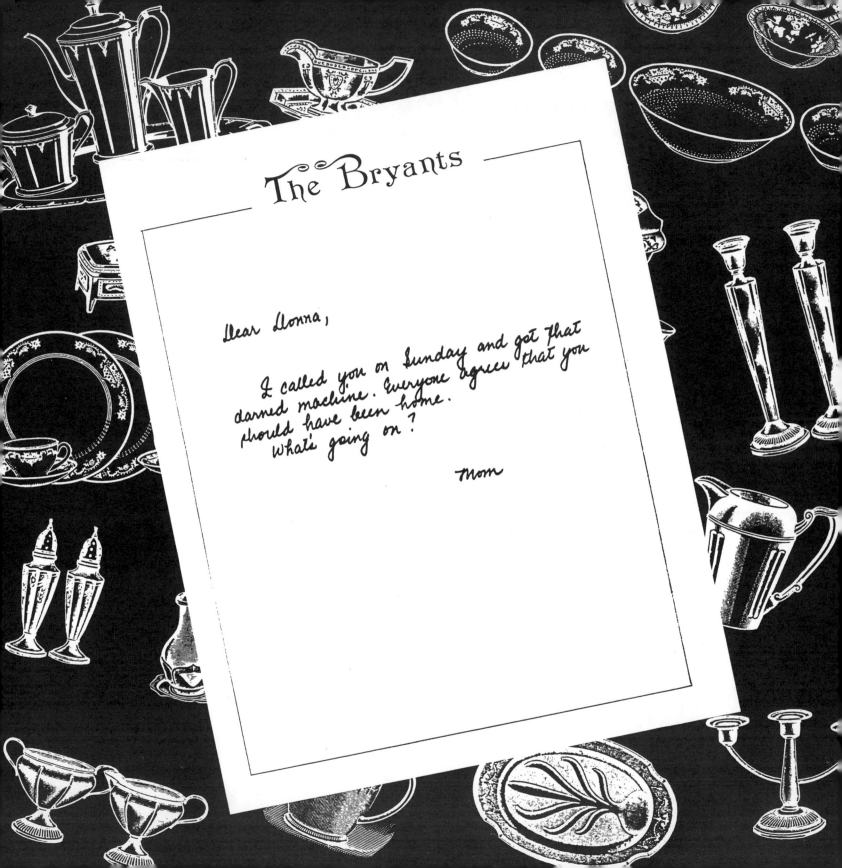

The Bryants

Dear Donna,

I called you on Sunday and got that darned machine. Everyone agrees that you should have been home. What's going on?

Mom

Pizza of Sliced Pork Called "Where Have You Been?"

You can only get decent meats on Mondays or Thursdays.

All-Purpose Pizza Dough for Mother's Day
  (see page 85)
2 butterfly pork chops
2 tablespoons olive oil
Teriyaki sauce to braise it
2 cloves garlic, crushed
Ground black pepper
Tomato Sauce I Would Name After You
  (see page 87)
1 yellow pepper, cleaned and sliced

Set your oven for 450 degrees while you do this.
Fry the pork chops in the oil, teriyaki sauce, garlic, and black pepper until done; then slice into narrow strips. If your phone rings during this process, go and answer it, don't just let the machine take a message. Add the pork strips into the tomato sauce, and cook for a few minutes to acquaint the flavors with each other. Then apply the sauce to the awaiting dough, and arrange the slices of yellow pepper on top. Bake for fifteen minutes.

SHEMP'S TEMPS

Dear Mom,

Sorry I missed you on Sunday. I was helping Xavier in the soup Kitchen at the shelter. Don't worry, I sterilized all my clothing and boiled my hair afterwards.

We have a lot in common, Xavier and I, and I can't wait until you meet him, I think.

Love,
Donna

From the desk of DONNA BRYANT

"You Call That a Date?"
Pizza of Prosciutto and Strawberries

All-Purpose Pizza Dough for Mother's Day
   (see page 85)
Pizza I Would Name After You
   (see page 87)
⅓ pound prosciutto, sliced thin
1 pint strawberries, cut into quarters
Juice of 1 lemon

*M*ake the Pizza I Would Name After You and let it cool. When you buy your prosciutto, don't just walk away while it's being sliced. You need to hover over them, or they just don't get it right. You don't want the very end piece, and you don't want it cut like lunch meat. It has to be veil thin. Tear this into pieces and drape about the cooled pizza. Toss the strawberries in the lemon juice and apply them to the top and serve.

The Bryants

Dear Donna,

What do you have against Americans anyway? And what happened to Nigel? Did he break up with you? Why won't you tell me? Everyone at the Club could have listened to that British accent all day.

Love,
Mom

International Pizza

You can always buy English muffins, if you get the ones in the refrigerator case. Otherwise, only get them on Mondays, unless you go to a bakery.

1 eggplant
4 tablespoons olive oil
1 clove garlic, crushed
1 red pepper
2 English muffins (4 halves)
1 teaspoon dried oregano

Warm your oven to 450 degrees while you prepare the vegetables.
You remember how to treat the eggplants? I'm not going to go through that again. Fry the thin slices of eggplant in half the oil and all the garlic until they are almost brown. Clean and slice the pepper, sprinkle it with the remaining oil, and broil it under a hot flame for five minutes. Brush the muffins with oil, then drape over with the eggplant and peppers and bake for fifteen minutes. Shake the oregano over them in the last five minutes.

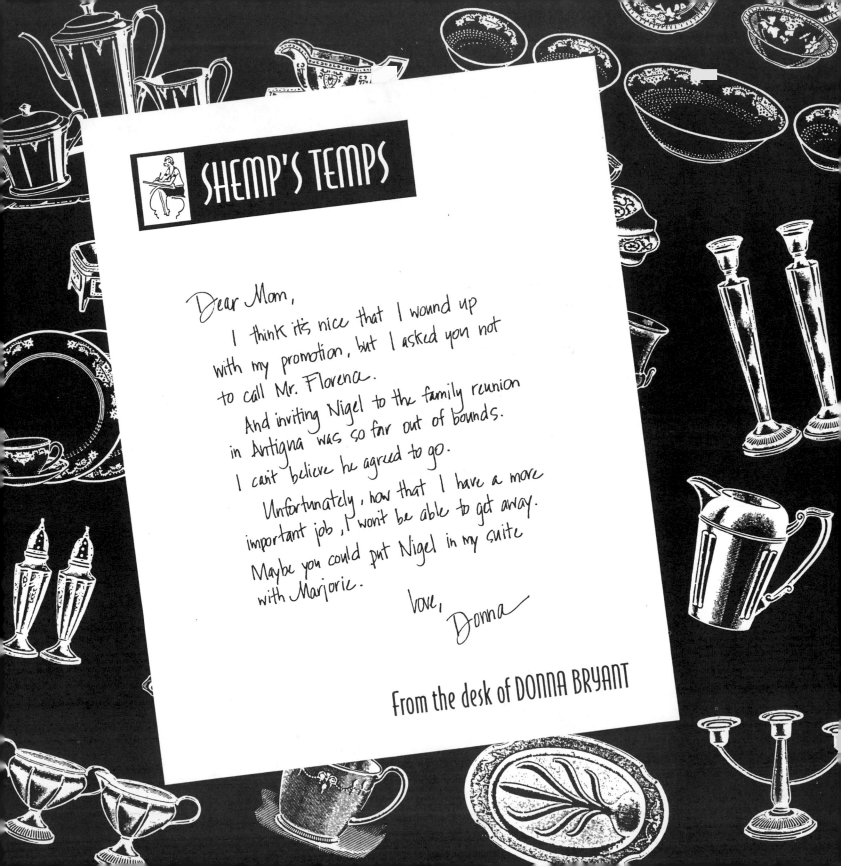

SHEMP'S TEMPS

Dear Mom,

I think it's nice that I wound up with my promotion, but I asked you not to call Mr. Florence.

And inviting Nigel to the family reunion in Antigua was so far out of bounds. I can't believe he agreed to go.

Unfortunately, now that I have a more important job, I won't be able to get away. Maybe you could put Nigel in my suite with Marjorie.

Love,
Donna

From the desk of DONNA BRYANT

Enough Egg Salad Pizza for a Family Reunion

Eggs sold in Styrofoam cartons aren't as high-quality as those in the cardboard ones, but they sell faster; so it makes me think they're probably fresher. You decide. I am fully aware that you are capable of making a lot of decisions on your own, you know.

All-Purpose Pizza Dough for Mother's Day,
   (see page 85)
1 white onion, minced
2 red potatoes, sliced thin
¼ cup olive oil
1 tomato, peeled, seeded, and minced
⅓ pound Genoa salami, sliced thin
⅓ pound mozzarella, sliced thin
4 to 6 pitted black olives, halved
3 eggs
Ground black pepper

*H*ave your oven ready at 450. Fry the onion and potatoes in the oil for five minutes, then bring in the tomato for another minute or two. Apply this to the pizza dough, and cover it with salami and mozzarella slices and olives. Bake for ten minutes. Beat the eggs with the ground pepper added and pour them over the top of the pizza to bake for another five minutes and serve.

Beauty Products
and
Erika and her Mother

"I cannot bear a mother's tears."
—Virgil

The story of a mother-daughter love that conquers the most insipid features of the popular culture, including its tendency to favor artificial beauty enhancers to the real thing.

ERIKA

Dear Mom,

OK, thanks. It was a good idea and everything.

But I had no idea everyone would be so old. That was just creepy.

The worst part was when he came out on the stand, which, by the way, wasn't decorated at all, and had the hairiest arms in the world. Just because he's Ferlinghetti doesn't mean people should have to know about his hairy arms.

I maybe could have stayed, except that I was with Turk, which doubled how embarrassing that hippie fest was.

Thanks anyway, Erika

Shampoo That Could Inspire a Poet

2 cups white wine
2 cups rose water
A few drops of oil of bergamot
The same amount of oil of cloves

Whites of 4 eggs

Prepare this potion first and set it aside for fourteen days. Like any poetic creation, you'll come back to it and it will seem better. Combine the wine, rose water, and oils. Cork them carefully in an opaque vessel for their resting time.

After the necessary days have passed, beat the eggs into a froth and settle them into your hair, attending especially to the roots. Take a rest, read a bit. When the eggs have dried, rinse your hair through with the potion. Follow with warm water.

Dear Erika,

I might have heard the poem that would change my life at a Jack Kerouac reading in Big Sur in 1962.

Every picnic was fragrant, and every star could have lit the whole night. But I was thinking that my dress had a full skirt, and A lines were coming into style. And I was worried that my bangs were too short.

Thank you for reminding me, "Thou art thy mother's glass and she in thee Calls back the lovely April of her prime."

Love,
Mother

A Facial Mask to Call Back
a Lovelier Time

1 quart rose water
4 egg whites, beaten
1 tablespoon talc (such as baby powder)
2 tablespoons almond oil

Heat the rose water in a little pan and fold in the beaten egg whites. Cook for a few minutes before inviting the next two items. Make this into a delicate paste, adding more talc or oil if needed. Wear this on your skin overnight for a renewed appearance and a reduction in wrinkles, as if you would ever see one.

ERIKA

Dear Mom,

Your letter is real confusing. I'm taking $40-
for Dax & stuff. Also, I need a credit card to
try to rent a car for the trip.

Thanks for offering yours, but I can't drive around
with those earth bumper stickers and not die
of humiliation.

Thanks, though
Love, Erika

A Refreshing Wash for a Journey

1 quart rainwater or, if you must, bottled water
6 drops oil of pimpernel or primrose oil or a big
    handful of pimpernel or primrose blossoms

*H*eat the water as if for tea, and steep your oil or flowers in the water in a steaming pot. Cover it tightly for a day or so; then use it as a formidable stimulant when your skin is weary.

ERIKA

Dear Mom,

Sorry I haven't called much. We'll be staying down here a few more days with Turk's parents. I partly hate it because it mostly sucks, but it's a vacation, and we go out for dinner every night to some big deal place with his wanna-be Candace Bergen and Richard Dreyfus parents.

The beaches are dorky, but get a little better at night. I've tried to have a couple of conversations with his Mom, but she reads every trendy book she can, and I'm just not into that. Books cost too much. They have good magazines here, though.

Tomorrow we're going shopping. I hope I don't have to try stuff on in front of her. I know she'll want to be trying on those Addams Family black tank dresses that the forty-somethings like to think make them look really svelte and timeless.

I guess I'm into some absent days at school by now, so get ready to write me a lot of notes.

Love, Erika

A Gentle Potion for Clarifying and Evening a Tan

1 cup cream
2 tablespoons lemon juice
2 tablespoons grappa, clear brandy, or sake
½ teaspoon cinnamon

*T*end this as if it were soup, heating the mixture and skimming away what rises to the top. Store it in the refrigerator and apply before you go under the Sun's rays. This potion encourages even tanning; wear it under your sunscreen.

A Wash for Skin So Clear It Could Distract Attention from Any Other Shortcoming

½ cup flour
½ cup white vinegar
½ cup white wine
4 egg yolks (you could use the leftover yolks
   from my shampoo recipe)
Several drops oil of spearmint

Combine the flour, vinegar, and wine and let them sit together for half a day or so; then stir in the egg yolks and spearmint oil. Store this in the refrigerator for about seven days. Apply after dark, then wash it away in the morning.

Dear Erika,

I didn't think this would happen again, because you're so grown up now; but I am lying awake about you lately. Sometimes, I pray you will make things easy for me and just stay a little child. Sometimes, I pray that I will surrender to your independence. Sometimes, I become vain and pray that you will remember that it was I who set you in motion.

I didn't have a boyfriend to fret about, and it's just possible that I'm envious. But that doesn't begin to mean that I don't realize that you are tormented somehow, and that Turk is much more important than I can know. I hope you have resolved your misunderstanding like the mature person that you are.

Forgive my indulgence if I pine once in a while for the days when you would pull on my clothes and beg for a little taste of something from the stove, a hundred million years ago; before you were a bold, brave woman.

Love,
Mother

A Bracing Wash to Inspire a Memory

Equal parts of strong chamomile tea,
    rose water, and grappa

*H*eat these ingredients in a ceramic pot for a little while. It's best if you don't let this creation boil. Let it cool in a quiet place, then store it in a glass vessel, tightly corked. Use this as a rinse after cleansing the face.

ERIKA

Dear Mom,

Thanks for the letter. It was really thick, and made Turk's parents think I'm literary. I just realized today that I'm having more fun with them than with Turk the Jerk. As you would say, our days are numbered.

What do you mean that you didn't have any boyfriends? What about Trent?

Love, Erika

An Overnight Treatment
for Elegant Hands

A cake of soap that you already love
¼ cup olive oil
1 white unscented candle

*M*elt the soap and oil over a very soft, low flame. Stir together with a wooden spoon. Drip a few drops of candle wax into the warming mixture. Let this cool somewhat, and apply to your hands before you sleep. When you awaken, notice how refined your signature has become, how carefully you hold a letter, how delicate the movements of your fingers.

Dear Erika,

What about Trent? Are you serious?

When I love you the most, I feel
grateful that Trent happened to me and
not to you, the same way I felt
watching you fall from your bike.
Let it happen to me instead, I
thought.

Love,
Mother

A Calming Mask of Seeds to Remind You of How Things Grow

A handful of each:
Sunflower seeds
Cantaloupe seeds
Cucumber seeds
Pumpkin seeds

A small amount of cream to add drop by
    drop
A few drops of oil of lemon

Grind your seeds to a powder using a mortar and pestle or a food processor, and work in drops of cream until you have found a paste. Invite in the lemon drops last. Apply this to your face and allow it to set for twenty minutes before rinsing.

ERIKA

Dear Mom,
It's funny that you should say that about not
wishing a loser like Trent on me. I was wondering
if people in the sixties, like maybe you, ~~had~~ had
to put up with guys like Turk all the time.
You know, guys who have really smelly clothes on, and
started having long hair because it was glamorous,
but then they keep it because they don't know what
else to do with it, and it just gets more disgusting
by the day. Guys who don't seem to have heard a
word you have said. Who always expect you to pay
on dates and treat it like they're complimenting you
by doing that.
Sometimes I think, I'll put up with this from him
because it's complicated to break up, but if I thought
anyone were ever treating you like that, I couldn't
bear the pain.

Love, Erika

An Anointing Oil to Fill Two Hearts

Equal parts of:
Primrose water
Elder flower water
Dry white wine

A few drops of musk oil

*H*eat these softly to combine them, then store mixture for several days in a tightly corked vessel. Use it as a toilet water. Nineteenth-century ladies thought this solution to expand the bosom, but I think it just expands the feelings in the heart.

Salads from the Antimom
with
Letters to Jeanine

*"All things are full of signs,
and it is a wise one who can learn
about one thing from another."*
—Plotinus

*I*n her book *Otherness, Motherness and Green and Yellow Leafy Vegetables*, Hovelfencer deals with the special complexities of stepmothering and its relationship to hydroponic gardening. Hence, we look to salad recipes to reveal this story.

Dear Genene,

I know your dad has already brought up this problem, but I'm also going to ask you myself to stop introducing me to people as your stepmother. I'm not even thirty-five yet, and I'm standing next to a grown woman who's calling me stepmom. I find it mortifying. I should think "this is my father's new wife." would do.

Please try to keep it in mind. There's a lot on our calendar this summer!

Sincerely,

Claudia

Asparagus and Prosciutto That Are Vaguely Related

I've never actually made this, but I saw it prepared on a behind-the-scenes restaurant tour of Venice.

18 stalks of asparagus
6 paper thin slices prosciutto
¼ cup olive oil
Juice of one lemon
Black pepper to taste

Steam the asparagus until tender, but never mushy, then trim them to three-inch lengths, using only the tenderest parts. You probably don't own an asparagus cooker. As you can imagine, that would be optimal.

Wrap clusters of three stems in each slice of prosciutto, and tie, if possible. Otherwise, anchor them with toothpicks.

Make a quick dressing of the oil, lemon, and pepper, and sprinkle over the platter just before serving.

Dear Jeneen,

Don't you think it would look better if you invited some sort of a date for your Dad's birthday party? The tables are set for couples, and it's just odd to have threes.

What about finally introducing us to that sculptor or glass blower? Artists are usually interesting for brief periods.

Sincerely,

Claudia

Cucumber Salad for Two

I've never actually made this, but I learned about it in a cooking class I sat in on when we were on our cruise to Aruba.

2 tablespoons sugar
½ cup boiling water
½ cup balsamic vinegar
2 cucumbers, peeled and diced
2 medium carrots, shredded
4 scallions, chopped
3 fresh mint leaves, chopped
½ cup bean sprouts
1 small tomato, peeled, seeded, and diced
1 teaspoon ground ginger root
1 clove garlic, crushed
Salt and black pepper to taste

Dissolve the sugar in the boiling water, then add the vinegar. Chill that combination for at least two hours. When the dressing is ready, assemble all the other ingredients, and toss together. You can double this and serve four, but trying to make it for three would be extremely difficult.

Dear Janine,

Your Dad just installed an office line in one of the guest rooms, and I was thinking that when you call, you should use that number. Then you won't have to worry that you're disturbing me when you phone us in the late evenings. You can just leave a message on the machine, and I'm sure your dad will check it regularly.

Sincerely,

Claudia

You-Can-Never-Be-Too-Impersonal
Potato Salad

I've never prepared this myself, but I saw someone make it at the Turnabout at Nadine's where the clients become the chefs for one night every spring.

8 red potatoes
1 clove garlic, crushed
Black pepper to taste
2 stalks celery
½ cup dried cherries
½ cup diced McIntosh apples
½ cup mayonnaise

Dice the potatoes and steam them until tender. Add garlic and pepper during that process. Chill until thoroughly cooled. Toss with the remaining ingredients, adding mayonnaise last. If any of this is confusing, you can address your questions to me in writing, or by calling my office number.

Dear Jinean,

The Memorial Day Gala is extremely important to me. I know your dad gave you two tickets, but I was wondering if you wouldn't mind coming unescorted. It's not that Raven embarrasses me, but I think you might want to be free to meet people.

It's formal, you know. And if you need any advice at all, I'm here. In fact, it might be a good idea for me to help you pick out a dress. I know you have plans to do that with your mother, but I sense that she doesn't go to these kinds of events very often.

Sincerely,

Claudia

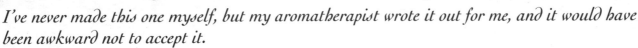

A Very Well Dressed Cauliflower Salad

I've never made this one myself, but my aromatherapist wrote it out for me, and it would have been awkward not to accept it.

1 head cauliflower
A bed of curly endive
3 hard-cooked eggs
Juice of one lemon
½ cup olive oil
Salt and black pepper to taste

Break the cauliflower into little flowerets, discarding the less than tender pieces. Steam them until just tender, but never mushy. Drain them, let them cook, and situate them on the bed of endive. Crumble the eggs into tiny pieces and mix in lemon juice, oil, salt, and pepper to use as a dressing for the salad.

Dear Vannean,

I can't believe you didn't go to your own graduation! I heard that you and your mother and that dreadful Raven were off somewhere sitting around and drinking wine! Do you realize that your father and I sat through four hours of speeches about preserving the stupid environment and seven hundred post adolescent losers' names being called so they could drag themselves across the gaudy stage to pick up their totally meaningless diplomas?

Your name got called, but nothing. We went through all that for absolutely no reason. I could have been at Lucien's for soft shell crab night, talking to some people who have lives.

Thanks again

CLAUDIA

Stimulating Crabmeat Salad for People Who Have Lives

This is a recipe I have never actually prepared, but a caterer left it behind at a party I recently held.

4 strips of well-cooked bacon
2 cups selected crabmeat
2 stalks celery, chopped
Juice of one lime
Mayonnaise
Black pepper to taste

There s no need to waste a lot of banter over this. Just put it all together. Crumble the bacon into the crabmeat, then add in the celery and dress with the lime juice, mayonnaise, and pepper.

Dear Jeanine,

We saw the review of your poetry reading in the paper today. Congratulations. I didn't even know you wrote poetry.

I used to write poetry once. I put it away because it was humiliating to wait tables and tend bar.

By the time I met your father I was fairly bitter about the artists' way, and I wanted a chance to be important. But seeing your review took my breath away. What a great time you must be having - everything I used to dream about - like-minded friends sitting very close together, drinking a little, laughing a lot because any little thing you do or say is understood by all the others. You're living out your real mission in life, and there's nothing to betray it.

I'd love to see your work. If you have a spare moment sometime, just call.

CLAUDIA

A Novice's Real Live Mayonnaise

This is my own recipe I've been making since I was in college.

6 teaspoons flour
1 cup boiling water
4 egg yolks
1 cup olive oil
1 cup balsamic vinegar
1 teaspoon salt

Slowly and carefully combine the flour and water in a pan, mixing until smooth. Then heat until a minute or two after boiling, and pour this over the egg yolks, which should be waiting in a glass bowl. Beat this until creamy, slowly bringing in the oil first, then the vinegar and salt, beating all the time.

You can vary this with a squeeze of lemon or lime, or a clove of crushed garlic. Store this in a glass container for up to three days.

Desserts from Clara

with

Letters to Lulu

~⊙~

"This is a time for action
because the future's within reach."
—Lou Reed

~⊙~

*T*he motivation to invent sweet things is a clear compensation for the basic and primitive sourness often discovered first in the mother-in-law model. And the use of eggs reminds us to ask, "Which came first, the mother or the mother-in-law?"

Dear Mother Clara,

Thank you so much for the package. It looked so happy, and full of surprises. The four tanks filled with Desert Storm soldiers and the seven GI Joes really made an impression on Oyeah. I kind of remember that we talked about steering him away from the military toys though. Do you remember?

Yours loving daughter-in-law,
Lu Lu

Thanks Again !!

A Little Birthday Cake
for a Little One

1 cup flour
1 cup brown sugar
½ cup ground cocoa
1 teaspoon baking powder
½ teaspoon baking soda
½ teaspoon salt
½ cup butter
1 cup cream
½ cup water
1 egg

Preheat your oven to 350. Combine all dry ingredients first, and blend them well. Then add in the butter, cream, water, and egg, and beat for a long time, as much as five minutes, with an electric blender. Pour into a greased cake pan or two greased loaf pans and bake for half hour. It's too bad there's so little sugar in this cake, but you can make up for it with frosting.

Dear Lulu-

I do like getting thank-you notes. They're very important, you know. I saw this in the paper, so I'm sending it along. No need to write back. You can get a free portrait session w/a haircut- but you need that coupon.

I know you're awfully busy- so I made Dylan's appointment for you. He looks like a girl! It's for Sept. 4th at 3:30, just after his nap. (I peeked at your calendar when I babysat- so I knew you were free.) Just order your own prints, because I already ordered mine.

Love,
Mother Clara.

Frosting That Looks Good Enough to Photograph for a Holiday Spread in Redbook

2 egg whites
1 teaspoon cream of tartar
1 cup sugar
¼ cup boiling water

Whip the egg whites with the cream of tartar until stiff, and slowly, slowly sprinkle in the sugar until it's all been added. Drip in the hot water as needed to make it spreadable, and keep whipping until it forms shiny peaks. Serve this almost immediately, because it dries out quickly. You'll have to plan your time more carefully than usual if you want to serve it at its peak.

Dear Mother Clara,

I noticed when you last babysat, Dylon seemed a little cronky at the end of the day, and had difficulty sleeping. Maybe he was just excited to get to play with you all day.

I did want to ask you about some empty packages that were sort of picking out of the garbage. Like, one was called Ridicu-Lick-yous, and the other, I can't believe it's Entirely Sugar. I think I remember mentioning when you brought the donuts for his breakfast that he probably shouldn't have much more sweet stuff that day.

Anyway, I just thought I could offer a friendly

Thanks Again!!

reminder that sugar really distresses him later on. Thank you so much for helping me out.

Your loving daughter-in-law,
Lu Lu

Emergency Chocolate Mousse You Can Make in Five Minutes

6 ounces chocolate chips
1 egg
½ cup milk
1 teaspoon almond extract
Just a pinch of salt

Away it goes, all into the blender. No problem. Just scald the milk first, all but boil it before you pour it in. Blend on high for a minute, then pour into your little serving cups and refrigerate for an hour before serving.

Desserts like this make it possible to eat something really rich pretty much every day.

Dear Lulu-

I was just over by my neighbor's to tell her that I got two thank-you notes from my daughter-in-law in as many weeks. Her daughter never writes- what a shame...

Well, as you're finding out, people who write thank-you notes get all the goodies.

Love,
Mother Clara

P.S. You forgot Dylan's haircut! I had to reschedule him for Sept. 18th- same time. They charged me a cancellation fee- but I'll just take it out of your birthday check.

Angel Food Cake for a Little Angel

6 egg whites
Few drops of ice water
½ teaspoon cream of tartar
¾ cup sugar
½ cup flour
½ teaspoon vanilla extract
½ teaspoon almond extract
Pinch of salt

*P*reheat your oven to 350. Be sure you don't have any other appointments before you get involved in this project. Add a few drops of ice water to the egg whites so that you can beat them into stiff peaks. Shake in the cream of tartar first. When the peaks are high and firm, add in the dry ingredients. It's easier if you sift the flour and sugar together a few times first. Add the extracts and salt last. Fold all this into a tube-style cake pan that you have greased and floured and bake for forty minutes.

Dear Clara,

I feel a little awkward bringing this up. You never ask, so I wonder if that means you just don't want to ask or you don't want to know. I wonder if Jamie is coming back too. I'm the one he left, after all. Maybe he left you too.

When he was around it was easy for you and me to get along because we could both relax. And now we are very nervous.

You might think I did something to drive him away. You might think I could have kept him around if I tried.

Think how far we have come only to know the privilege of caring for the same child together. Isn't that worth crawling about in this confusion?

Love,
LuLu

Free-Floating Meringues Like a Burden Lifted

6 egg whites
2 cups sugar, sifted several times
1 tablespoon baking powder
1 teaspoon vanilla extract

Preheat your oven to 300. Wait until your children have gone to bed before you use the mixer this much. What if you were beating eggs and couldn't hear them over the mixer, and they were setting fires or falling out the window? Beat the egg whites until stiff, and slowly fold in the sugar and baking powder. Drop in the vanilla last. Bake these in little dollops on brown paper spread on a baking sheet for about one hour. A nice variation is to fold in shredded coconut before baking.

Index